Mom's Garden

A Coloring Book for Mother's Day

Dear Colorists,

I am thrilled to present to you this beautiful coloring book featuring moms in the garden. This book is a celebration of the peace and joy that can be found in nature when you just need a moment of quiet.

In this coloring book, you will find delightful illustrations of mothers enjoying the beauty of the garden. Each page has intricate designs and details that will allow you to unleash your creativity and imagination.

As you color, you can imagine the warmth of the sun on your face, the scent of blooming flowers, and the gentle breeze rustling through the trees. You can picture yourself spending quality time in your happy place.

Whether you are looking for a fun activity to enjoy with your child or a unique gift to give to your mother, this coloring book is a perfect choice.

I hope this coloring book will bring you many hours of relaxation, creativity, and joy.

Let the colors of the garden inspire you, and let the love of motherhood shine through.

Happy coloring!